Male-reflective Christian theology is curiously unrepentant for the blatant way Christianity has been constructed "in the image of him."

What I am calling for is another Reformation of Christendom, freeing us this time not from the power of pope and priest but from the power of patriarchal males whatever their position.

To urge this is to challenge nearly everything in our tradition.

Feminism is God's call to us in this generation to open up to radical change so our tradition may be true again to Jesus, and become life-affirming for all.

SUNDAY SCHOOL MANIFESTO

In the Image of her?

•

Elizabeth Dodson Gray

ELIZABETH DODSON GRAY

Roundtable Press • Wellesley, Massachusetts

This is a reprint of Elizabeth Dodson Gray's chapter in
Theologies of Religious Education, edited by Randolph Crump Miller
and published by Religious Education Press (1995). Used with the permission of
Religious Education Press, Inc., 5316 Meadow Brook Road, Birmingham, AL 35242

Cover: Pablo Picasso, "Fleurs et Mains"
© 1994 Artists Rights Society (ARS), New York / SPADEM, Paris
Reproduced with the permission of ARS.

Drawings by Elizabeth Gibson Ferry were originally created for the flyers of the
Theological Opportunities Program at Harvard Divinity School, 1973-1994,
and are reproduced with the permission of the artist.

Photographs by Claire Flanders originally appeared in
No Hidden Meanings: An Illustrated Escatalogical Laundry List along with text by Sheldon Kopp
(Palo Alto, CA: Science & Behavior Books, Inc., 1975)
and are reproduced with the permission of the artist and the publisher.

Library of Congress Catalog Card Number: 94-67112
ISBN 0-934512-07-8

Dedicated to my daughter Lisa
and my granddaughters Tricia and Marie
and to the next generations
of
women and men, girls and boys

who deserve better
from our Christian tradition

Contents

4. Jesus' Crucifixion　　　　　　　　　43

Making Jesus into a "Salvation Machine" / The "Blood on the Cross" Message of Individual Salvation / A "Double Whammy" for Women / Seeing "That Old Rugged Cross" in a New Light / Creating a Fascination with Violence and Pain

5. Changing an Entire Tradition　　　　52

Making Women Visible / Cleansing the Temple / A Church Where Women Are Visible and Honored / Where Women Are Major Figures, Not Mere Bystanders / Church Life as a Massive "Latent Curriculum" / A Celebration of Women / Changing a Tradition of Celebrating Men / Going Beyond the Ancient and Crippling Hatred of Women / A Life-Affirming Tradition for Ourselves and Our Children / Can We Leave Behind Hierarchy? / Fruits of the Patriarchal Spirit / "I Was Just A Child" / Another Reformation

Notes　　　　　　　　　　　　　76

1.

Theology through "Male-Colored" Glasses

The Challenge of Feminism

Feminist theology is not one possible theology among a pantheon of male theologies. Feminism is such a drastic critique of the entire Christian tradition that it calls for the almost total recasting of that tradition and the reconstruing of its history.

Feminism points out the obvious but previously overlooked fact that Christianity is one of the many religious traditions in which it has been the males who have "named the sacred" from the viewing point of their own male life experience. Like Narcissus of Greek mythology, the male has looked into a pool which has made the religious tradition a reflection of himself.

This is what feminists mean when they call the received tradition "androcentric": it embodies the perception of the entire world through "male-colored" glasses. The absurdity of this interpretation of the human situation usually eludes us, until we realize that it is like left-handed or brown-eyed people assuming that their brown eyes or left-handedness gave them the only "keys to the kingdom."

The Power to Name How Things "Are"

Adam in the Genesis story is portrayed as "naming all the animals." This is an elegant parable to convey the truth that infant humans, female and male, are born into a whole social construction of reality done from the standing point of the male body and the male life experience. Of their socially-dominant gender the generic male can say, like Adam, "Everything is named, everything is thought, from *my* point of view." And all of us, having been born ""into and socialized within this "Adam's world," feel what patriarchal history for centuries said: "This is the way the world really *is,* " for we have never experienced life another way.

Our language itself reflects Adam's world. So-called "generic" language has perpetuated the illusion that all of the human species is made visible in the words *man* and *mankind.* Our

Michelangelo, THE CREATION OF ADAM. Sistine Chapel, Vatican State.

language is like a Rorschach test, imaging back to us reflections of even uniquely male genital experience in statements such as "the *thrust* of his thinking," "a *penetrating* statement," "a *seminal* book," even "*seminars.*" Yet male consciousness, like the Washington Monument to "the father of our country," has left us blissfully unaware of the frequently phallic nature of the sculpting of its monuments as well as its words.

In the long history of thought, Adam's world has given us male-constructed philosophy, male-constructed psychology, and, yes, male-constructed theology. It has been men who have

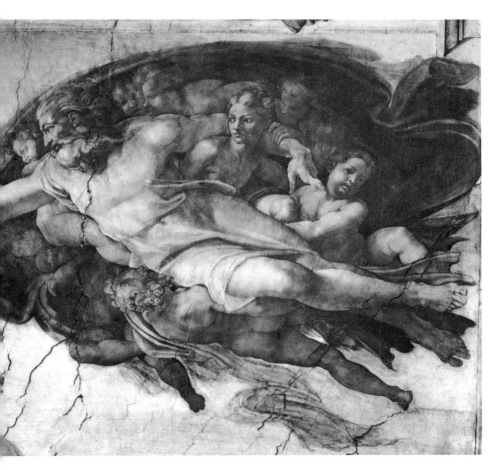

Alinari/Art Resource, NY

"erected" these great conceptual systems. Thus traditional Christian theology has imaged the generic human in the form of the male, and also imaged the divine in the form of the male. Michelangelo's portrayal of a bearded God reaching out the finger of creation-energy to fill Adam with life has been accepted in Western culture as an icon, a visual summary, of the theological statement that "God created man in His own image."

But when we take account of the sociology of knowledge, and notice *who* is *doing the knowing,* we realize that the "flow of creation" really happened as the *reverse* of what we earlier perceived. It is actually the human male who has created God in *his* own image. Yes, like Narcissus of old, the male sees only himself in the cosmic reflecting pool of ultimate mystery.

Unrepentant Male-Reflective Christian Theology

The feminist theologian Mary Daly says somewhere that when God is male, then the male is God. The sociologist Peter Berger writes, "Religion legitimates social institutions by bestowing upon them an ultimately valid ontological status, that is, by *locating* them within a sacred and cosmic frame of reference."[1] What Daly and Berger are saying is that when ultimate reality is imaged as being male, then male power—expressed in male political leaders, male corporate CEOs, and males as "heads" of patriarchal families—is made to seem credible and "natural."

So male-reflective Christian theology is not innocent. It is deeply implicated in the history of the creation of patriarchal structures of male power in the home and in church, and in legitimating the structures of economic, political and social power in the wider culture. Feminist scholars, from Mary Daly to Rosemary Radford Ruether to Elisabeth Schüssler Fiorenza to dozens of others, have written and published on these themes.[2]

But male Christian theology still seems curiously unrepentant for the blatant way Christianity has been constructed "in the

Michelangelo Caravaggio, NARCISSUS.
Alinari/Art Resource, NY

image of him."[3] This leaves Christian women, as in the lament of the ancient Hebrews, "singing their song in a strange land," a land not their own.

2.

The Denigration of Women

The Mark of the Divine

Christian piety and theology have always taken for granted that we humans are created in the image of God (Gen. 1:26). This has been the starting point for Christian self-understanding of our humanness, that somehow we bear the mark (or image) of the divine. Such theology in recent decades has undergone a feminist deconstruction exposing its roots in male perspectives and self-interest. Nonetheless we must recognize that this "image of God" theology has been extremely important over the centuries to the Christian church and to the Western world in constructing how various kinds of humans were "named," labeled, and thought about.

But women's problem with the Christian tradition is not just that it is all "in the image of him." It is also that from this male standing point, women were named as Other, as inferior, evil, unclean, "grotesque." So it is important that we examine more closely just how this denigration of women developed over the centuries and was articulated theologically.

Are Women Also in the Image of God?

Jane Dempsey Douglass, professor of historical theology at Princeton Theological Seminary, raises an interesting question: "Why," she asks, "did the doctrine of the image of God in all humanity not serve in the past to break down distinctions based upon gender and race?"[1]

Answering that question, she points out that from the very early years of the Christian era "theologians have taught that humanity was created in the image of God. But they have seemed ill at ease explaining how *women* bear that image. Adam is seen as created in the image of God, a God who is seen as man-like, or as having no gender. But when human sexual differentiation is taken into account, the image becomes problematic."

Over the centuries there has been a continuing struggle in Christian theological circles over how to explain that women also are made in the image of God. Douglass points out that strongly contributing to this difficulty was what the apostle Paul wrote in 1 Cor. 11:7b–9, "Man is the image and reflection of God, but woman is the reflection of man. Indeed, man was not made from woman, but woman from man. Neither was man created for the sake of woman, but woman for the sake of man" (NRSV).

"Some of the Church Fathers, like Gregory of Nyssa (b. c325) and Augustine (354–430), developed double-creation schemes. There was a purely spiritual creation of humanity (Gen. 1) before there was the creation of bodily differentiation (Gen. 2). But then," says Douglass, "having done this, the female was then seen as reflecting the image of God *less fully* than the male because of her different and inferior bodily nature."

Douglass reports that Chrysostom (c.345–407) and other Eastern Mediterranean theologians working out of Antioch "lean heavily on 1 Cor 11:7 to argue that 'ruling' and 'governance' are a critical part of the image of God. And it is men that are endowed with that capacity to imitate God's ruling. Again this view militates against the fullness of God's image in women," observes Douglass.

Pronouncing Women Inferior

It turns out that Aristotle (384–322 BC) is quite important in this discussion about women and the image of God. It was Aristotle who had said: "The female is a female by virtue of a certain lack of qualities—a natural defectiveness—a 'misbegotten male'" (*On the Generation of Animals 2, 3*).

Uta Ranke-Heinemann is professor of the history of religion at the University of Essen. In *Eunuchs for the Kingdom of Heaven: Women, Sexuality and the Catholic Church* she writes: "These belittling notions of woman as a kind of flower pot for the male's semen were worked up by Aristotle into a theory that lasted for thousands of years. Aristotle, Albertus Magnus, and Thomas Aquinas see things this way: According to the basic principle that 'Every active element creates something like itself,' only men should actually be born from copulation. The energy in semen aims of itself to produce something equally perfect, namely, another man. But owing to unfavorable circumstances women, i.e., misbegotten men, come into existence. Aristotle calls woman *'arren peperomenon,'* a mutilated or imperfect male."[2] She continues: "Thomas says that women do not correspond to 'nature's first intention,' which aims at perfection (men), but to 'nature's second intention, (to such things as) decay, deformity, and the weakness of age' (*Summa Theologiae* I q. 52 a. 1 ad 2)."[3]

Nine centuries after Aristotle's death, in the year 585 AD, a gathering assembled in a general Council for all of France, the second Synod of Mâcon. Forty-three Christian bishops and twenty men representing other bishops debated, among other things, a most peculiar topic: "Are women human and fully 'person' (*homo*)?" When a vote was finally taken, in the infinite wisdom of the males present, women were officially declared human![4]

Margaret Miles, professor of historical theology at Harvard Divinity School, writes of this discussion still being carried on in the Middle Ages. In *Carnal Knowing: Female Nakedness and Religious Meaning in the Christian West* she says, "In the Middle Ages Aristotle's doctrine of woman as a misbegotten and deformed male crossed easily into Christian speculation about Eve and her secondary and derivative creation."[5] After all, it was said, God created Adam first, so women must be second-best.

Thus Christian theology functioned for centuries as a potent cultural force declaring women inferior beings. You might think this was surely sufficient denigrating to do to one half of the human species—the half that conceives and bears the next human generation. But no, Christian theology went further, declaring women to be evil, defiling, dangerous, even grotesque.

Proclaiming Women Evil

Using the powerful negative image of Eve, the one who "led Adam" into disobedience and so the one by whom sin came into the world, women were portrayed by generations of Christian theologians as both inheritors and perpetuators of human evil and disobedience.

Tertullian (c160-c230) said: "Do you know that each of you women is an Eve? . . . You are the gate of Hell ['the devil's gateway,' it is sometimes translated], you are the temptress of the forbidden tree, you are the first deserter of the divine law."[6] Echoes of Tertullian's words persist in Christian thought of subsequent centuries.

Medieval "theologians, philosophers and medical authors discussed the question of whether woman is a 'monstrous creation.'"[7] Of this discussion Margaret Miles says: "Figured as Eve, the perversely bent rib, every woman was seen as essentially grotesque, though the revelation of her hidden monstrosity could be prevented by her careful adherence to socially approved appearance and behavior."[8]

"One of the most prominent features of the grotesque," writes Miles, "is sexuality and the sexual organs, and female reproductive functions, as we will see, were in the medieval period the quintessential terror that must be 'conquered by laughter.'" She cites the work of Michel Bakhtin, one of the major scholars of the grotesque. "Bakhtin identifies the three main acts in the life of the grotesque body as 'sexual intercourse, death throes, and the act of birth.' 'Birth and death are the gaping jaws of the earth and the mother's open womb.'"[9]

In the medieval world, Miles says, "Pregnancy and birth provide images of 'natural' grotesqueness. 'Woman with child is a revolting spectacle,' Jerome wrote in the fourth century, a judgment with which countless medieval authors concurred. Pregnancy, like menstruation," writes Miles, "reveals that a woman's body is not the 'closed, smooth, and impenetrable' body that serves as the symbol of individual, autonomous, and 'perfect' existence. In menstruation, sexual intercourse, and pregnancy, women's bodies lose their individual configuration and boundaries."[10]

In both Judaism and Christianity women were declared befouled and contaminated by our natural body functions of menstruation and childbirth. A woman was so contaminating of the sacred liturgical space presided over by male priests that a woman was exiled or banned during times of menstruation and birth and required to undergo a special cleansing ritual before she could be allowed back into the sacred space of worship.[11]

Deciding Sexual Intercourse with Women Is Evil

But here the Christian theologians have created a problem for the heterosexual male.[12] If women and women's bodies are so horrible and defiling, then what about men having sexual intercourse with women?

In his book *Power and Sexuality: The Emergence of Canon Law at the Synod of Elvira,* historical theologian Samuel Laeuchli examines how church leaders in Spain in 309 at the Synod of Elvira for the first time created an explicitly antisexual code and called upon men to rise spiritually above their sexual bodies. "In the image of manhood which these canons presuppose, the woman as a sexual being was excluded."[13] "[S]exuality," says Laeuchli, "becomes synonymous with evil. The sexual act becomes abhorrent and people either flee into deserts or write

Elizabeth Gibson Ferry

books on the perfection of virginity."[14]

But it was Augustine (354–430) in his *Confessions* who gave these anti-sexual views what was to be their classic formulation.[15] Augustine wrote of *concupiscence*, or what is usually translated "sexual desire" or "lust." He proposed a biological theory about the transmission of original sin from one generation to the next. Augustine was speaking to the problem of how Eve's sin could be our sin. How could her sin be transmitted to us? His answer was *concupiscence* or lust. In the act of sexual intercourse, something spoils the act (and indeed spoils the whole human race). That something was and is sexual desire.

What Augustine was building was a theological case for the necessity of baptism. Baptism, he said, washes away that original sin transmitted to us from our parents' sexual desire. Baptism, then, is the recommended spiritual cleanser for bleaching out the stain caused by our parents' erotic impulses at the time of our conception. So baptism is his solution to a problem which Augustine himself created. It was a sort of spiritual antibiotic, cleverly constructed to match the lethal "virus" he had theologically conjured up.

So here is a Catch-22, a religious system created by men that labels our women's bodies so carnal and sexual and evil that normal heterosexual desire for women finally contaminates both the men and their children. Note however that women may procreate without experiencing any sexual desire. Since it is males who must experience such desire in order to become erect and ejaculate, what Augustine has created theologically becomes a formidable problem for the Christian heterosexual male. Augustine has, in effect, launched a powerful theological boomerang, one that returns to wound whatever male uses it.

But there was a way to avoid this wounding, and males for centuries have used their standing point as "the namer" to avoid taking responsibility for their own sexuality. They have done this by psychological projection, disowning their own sexual desires and erotic imagination, and projecting them "out" onto women.

Elizabeth Gibson Ferry

For generations men were able to blame women as the source of all "carnal desire," and in this way they avoided facing up to their own lustful fantasies and whatever it was that they as males were doing with their own sexuality. Thus they neatly avoided taking any responsibility, and viewed women instead as the source of this now-declared evil. "All witchcraft comes from carnal desire, *desire which in women is insatiable."* wrote the authors of *The Hammer of Witches* in 1487 just after the start of the Inquisition.[16] It is difficult for us today to read that pronouncement with a straight face. In court records in the United States today there are literally thousands of cases of rape, incest and pedophilia by males.[17] There is a minuscule record of such offenses perpetrated by women. "Insatiable carnal lust" *in women?*—who do we think we're kidding?[18]

The Culpability of the Christian Tradition

Feminist scholars Jane Dempsey Douglass, Carter Heyward, Margaret Miles, and Uta Ranke-Heinemann, among others, have dug deep into the literary records of the Christian tradition and unearthed these terrible anti-sexual and anti-woman pronouncements. Their scholarship helps women today understand that the difficulties women may have with self-esteem, self-confidence and self-assertion are more than just their own individual or personal issues. These issues are culture-wide. They are widely shared wounds, which trace their origin to messages about women promulgated continuously and with great priority and intensity throughout the long history of our Christian tradition.

Feminists have concluded that *Christianity's contempt for women and their bodies has been an essential backdrop legitimating the violence against women.* Rosemary Radford Ruether, for example, says: "Historical Christianity defined women as inferior, subordinate, and prone to the demonic. These images justified almost limitless violence against them whenever they crossed the male will at home or in society. Woman as

Elizabeth Gibson Ferry

victim is the underside of patriarchal history. . . . "[19]

The full extent, intensity and duration of this violence toward women is only now being unearthed by feminist scholars. During "the Witch-Burnings," hundreds of thousands of women were burned at the stake (or drowned) as witches. This continued for more than two centuries (1484–1692) in the Catholic and Protestant Christian West. In addition, evidence in literary and ecclesiastical records shows there have always been the violent assaults of incest, child abuse, wife-battering, religiously sanctioned child-beating, marital rape, acquaintance rape, stranger rape, war rape, and individual killings of women.[20]

All these forms of violence create and sustain a theologically and religiously sanctioned culture of ongoing oppression into which women are born, grow up, and expected to find a place, their "woman's place." In other cultures the violence toward women has its roots in different (but still male) social and religious traditions. But in the Christian West such violence is rooted in the denigration of women which is powerfully and continuously articulated by the Christian anti-woman and anti-sex tradition. It is important we be clear in our own minds that in all this violence, *the perpetrators are not just individual males who are violent. It is the entire tradition which is culpable of doing structural, theological violence to women.*

Because it has been the entire tradition, it is very important now that the entire tradition genuinely and explicitly repent for this violent and damaging patriarchal past and for all the hurt it has caused women. I want this repentance to be "out loud," articulated loudly and clearly in our regular church services and in our church pronouncements. And I want change.

Elizabeth Gibson Ferry

3.

Jesus and Women

Jesus' Radical Affirmation of Women

The Christian tradition as it developed in the centuries after Jesus has been woman-hating. Yet if one looks to some of that tradition's earliest written materials—the four gospels about Jesus' life—no greater contrast to this woman-hating Christian tradition can be imagined than Jesus' own interactions with women. Rachel Conrad Wahlberg[1] has focused on these interactions, and it is she who has given me fresh eyes to see that Jesus is not only *not* woman-hating, but in the gospel accounts of his words and actions he is radically woman-*affirming* in ways totally at odds with both his own time and with the subsequent Christian tradition.

When I was growing up as a Southern Baptist my reading of the gospels was supplemented in sermons by briefings on certain aspects of Jesus' social context. But other aspects of that social context were never discussed. For example, I learned that in order to understand the gospel account of Jesus' conversation with the Samaritan woman at the well (John 4:7–30), I needed to be aware of the tradition of enmity between Jews and Samaritans.

What was *not* discussed was the traditional customs governing conversations between men and women in that day. Jesus and all men were prohibited by social custom from speaking to women not already known to them.[2] So I never really saw how radical a social departure Jesus' conversation at the well really was.

Truly "Disciples," Not First-Century Groupies

Women, unless accompanied by a man, were also enjoined by social custom to stay in the immediate surroundings of their own home.[3] Without awareness of these social customs, I lacked the background to understand or appreciate the life-transforming commitment being made by the women who "followed" Jesus as he traveled (Luke 8:1-3). They were truly "disciples," not first-century Palestinian groupies or hangers-on.

I was instructed, for example, in the Sabbath rules of Judaism. I had to understand these to grasp the explosive impact of Jesus' actions as he "broke" Sabbath rules. But I never heard in child-hood sermon or seminary classroom about similar rules and customs narrowing the worlds of women in New Testament times. So I was unprepared to understand the equally explosive impact Jesus had when he disregarded the conventions governing male/female relationships in his day.

For example, Jesus talks *theology* with the woman at the well. He did this at a time when men not only did not talk to women in public but women were not allowed to study the Torah. This must have meant that women were always excluded as participants in religious discourse. But when Jesus visits Mary and Martha, he encourages Mary to leave Martha in the kitchen and join the men in talking theology (Luke 10:38–42). Later, after the death of their brother Lazarus, Jesus does not rebuke Martha for upbraiding him for his being absent and thus unable to heal her brother in his mortal illness. Instead Jesus engages now Martha (who earlier had been the one who labored in the kitchen) in a serious theological discussion of death and resurrection, saying finally, "*I* am the resurrection and the life" (John 11:1–26).

Women as Hearers and Doers of the Word of God

When a woman from a crowd shouts out her affirmation of his mother's womb and breasts—"Blessed is the womb that bore you, and the breasts that you sucked!" (Luke 11:27–28)—Jesus responds with the amazing affirmation that a woman is more than her uterus, indeed more than her reproductive function.[4]

In a time when women gained social value for having children and especially male children, and were seriously devalued for being "barren,"[5] it was a radical thing for Jesus to reject the image of woman as a biological and reproductive vessel only. Jesus is affirming that a woman is also a serious "choosing" human agent who can choose to "hear the word of God and do it" (Luke 11:28). Women are affirmed as Hearer and Doer of the Word.[6]

So after our Christian churches repent of all the woman-hating in our Christian tradition, something else I want is the preaching, the educational activities, and all of local church life to make crystal-clear to children (and to everyone) just how radically *woman-affirming* the churches' founder, Jesus, really was.

Jesus and the Apostolic Role of Women

A great deal has always been made within Christianity about being an apostle (see 1 Cor. 15:3–11) and the apostolic commission of "Go and tell." An apostle is someone who is sent, usually with the "apostolic" task of going and preaching, or proclaiming the good news of Jesus.

It seems to have escaped the serious attention of a male-obsessed tradition that women were the very first apostles, the first to be commissioned by Jesus himself to go and tell. It is to the woman at the well that Jesus first says he is the Messiah: "I who speak to you am he" (John 4:26). She then, the gospel says, goes and tells other people so convincingly that they *believe* (John 4:28–30)! Thus this woman at the well *is an apostle,* perhaps the first preacher of Jesus as the Messiah.

Equally surprising is how the Christian tradition from as early as we can glimpse it (1 Cor. 15:5) has downplayed the "apostolic" role of women in the resurrection narratives. But women are the first witnesses of Jesus' resurrection (Mark 16:1–8; Matt. 28:1–

Elizabeth Gibson Ferry

10; Luke 24:1–11). And here in these resurrection narratives those same words of apostolic commission occur. In Mark 16:7 the angel says to the women, *"Go and tell* his disciples"; in Matt. 28:8, "They ran *to tell"*; in Luke 24:9, "They *told* this to the eleven"; and in John 20:14–18, when Mary Magdalene sees Jesus outside the empty tomb and mistakes him for a gardener, Jesus again says, *"Go and tell* the others." Women are "sent" as apostles by Jesus!

But for the Faithfulness of These Women . . .

Had it not been for these women's faithfulness, there would not be an Easter morning account of the resurrection, since the male disciples had all run away and did not come to the tomb. And when the women told Jesus' male followers of their experience of him raised from the dead, the men would not even believe the women—"but these words seemed to them an idle tale, and they did not believe them" (Luke 24:11). The gospel traditions let us glimpse the fact that even at this critical juncture the women were not believed, nor were they viewed as credible witnesses.

This may be why Paul, trying to be convincing to Christians at Corinth about Christ's resurrection and his own apostolic credentials, does not mention the risen Christ's Easter appearances to the women. Certainly these Easter appearances first of all to women would certainly never have been created later by pious tradition[7] because these accounts were so truly counter-cultural. Furthermore, like Peter's denial, they cast in a bad light the male disciples who later became leaders in the earliest Christian communities. So, precisely because they are *not* what a pious male-dominated tradition would have found congenial or useful, these accounts are undoubtedly authentic.

Jesus' Use of Female Metaphors to Speak of God

Look also at the images for God which Jesus is recorded in the gospels as using. Everyone touched by the Christian tradition has heard a lot about God (and Jesus) as "the good shepherd." The God-as-shepherd image has become an icon, and is celebrated in innumerable stained glass windows. Likewise we all know the story of "the prodigal son" and its related image of God-as-loving-Father grieving a lost son.

But both of these oft-repeated and oft-pictured images for God occur in the same chapter of Luke's gospel (Luke 15) alongside another image of God which Jesus used, an image of God as like a woman (Luke 15:8–9). This latter image is scarcely ever referred to in prayer or sermon nor is it portrayed in stained glass as an icon suitable for contemplation and comfort. This is the story of the woman with the lost coin.

The common theme in Luke 15 is lostness and foundness: a lost sheep, a lost coin, a lost son. Each time what has been lost is found, and the words of the refrain echo each other: "Rejoice with me, for I have found my coin (my sheep, my son) which I had lost. Even so I tell you, there is joy before the angels of God [in heaven] over one sinner who repents."

The Absurdity of the "Maleness" of God

It is not simply that in Luke 15 Jesus is recorded as giving his hearers a female God-image, an image which has been largely ignored throughout Christian history. It is also that *Jesus himself was gender-inclusive in his own chosen God-images.* This renders rather absurd our contemporary debates about the maleness of God and the use of gender-inclusive language about God. It indicates instead that we have not really "seen" the biblical Jesus as he appears in the gospels. The truth is that *the male-obsessed church through the ages has restricted our symbolic universe to only male God-images in language and story,* something the gospels indicate Jesus himself never did.

There are also probably no stained glass windows commemorating Jesus' image of himself as a mother hen (Luke 13:34, Matt. 23:37). Here Jesus suggests he is like a *female* parent, even a female *animal* parent, who is gathering her offspring under her wings. This image of Jesus also is clearly neglected by the male-

Marion C. Honors, CSJ, GOD-IMAGE WOMAN. Permission of the artist.

dominated Christian tradition because it did not fit their idealized image of Jesus as the God-man. Can you imagine such a one as a mother-hen? Apparently Jesus could.

Reproductive Blood and Birth: Contaminating or Sacred?

Jesus lived in a religious culture which declared women "unclean" or religiously polluted and polluting when they menstruate or after they give birth. It is interesting how Jesus responds when he himself is made "unclean" (according to that culture) because he has been simply touched (and hence "polluted") by the woman with the issue of blood which has been on-going in her for many years (Mark 5:24–34).

Jesus did not rebuke her for touching him and making him unclean. Nor did he pull away from her or send her away. Instead she was healed, and Jesus told her to go in peace. So Jesus also breaks decisively with the taboo of women's uncleanness.[8]

Because Jesus grew up in a religious culture which had named women's natural process of giving birth as unclean and defiling of sacred space, he must have learned those attitudes about women's bodies, menstruating, and giving birth. Yet when Jesus chose a metaphor for spiritual conversion and transformation, he chose *giving birth* (John 3:3–8 only). How remarkable![9]

When Jesus uses the birth image as the metaphor for "coming into new life in the spirit," there is respect and reverence in his words for the birth process which women experience. How could subsequent Christian tradition hallow those words "born again" into a very influential theological formula, yet still continue in Roman Catholic and Episcopal liturgical menus to keep the women-denigrating "cleansing" services until the 1970s? Jesus' respect for the birth-process was not able to be translated into the male-obsessed tradition but was instead spiritualized so that the theological denigration of women's actual bodies could be continued.

The Jesus Who Is Respectful of Women's Bodies and Minds

What do I conclude from all this in the gospel accounts about Jesus and women? I conclude that Jesus is a good model for full adult relationships—a model which unfortunately the male-dominated church was unable to follow but instead chose to abandon.

Jesus alone among the men in the gospel record did not accept the first-century mold for women. He took women as seriously as he took men. He never patronized women or demeaned them[10] or constricted them to "their place" as defined by the social conventions of his day. He rejected stereotyping women as "birth vessels" or kitchen helpers. He used female images for God and for himself, and he chose as his metaphor for conversion women's unclean birth process: "being born anew" or again.

Jesus treated women, women's bodies, and women's life-processes *respectfully.* Can you imagine what Jesus' reaction would be today to the worldwide epidemic of violence against women in the forms of pornography, rape, incest, battering, war rape, and murder? Then, ask yourself, Have you ever heard from the pulpit such a sermon—about Jesus' reaction to present-day violence against women?

Jesus was respectful of women's minds. He talked serious theology to them about the Messiah and the resurrection. He is respectful of women's spiritual capacities, which responded to his life and message, and he repeatedly gives women the apostolic commission to "go and tell."

Tampering with the Evidence

That women were active in this role in the earliest Christian communities is testified to by Paul who in Romans 16:7 names a person, for centuries referred to by the male name *Junias,* as "prominent among the apostles" and "in Christ before I was." The story of the naming of that person is a cautionary tale, because a woman-denigrating tradition was reworking the evidence in subsequent centuries.

For approximately the last millennia it has been assumed that Paul's words referred to a male apostle. But in very recent years Bernadette Brooten, while reading John Chrysostom's *Commentary on Romans* (written late in the 4th century—his dates are 345?–407), noticed that Chrysostom wrote of there being a *woman* apostle, *Junia.* "To be an apostle," he wrote, "is something great. . . . How great the wisdom of *this woman* must have been" (emphasis added).

Brooten realized she had made a truly exciting discovery—the presence of corroborating non-scriptural evidence from the early centuries that *they* knew then that there had been at least one women apostle in earliest Christianity.[11] This is shocking to us only because for the last 1000 years or so (she found) the church has said (and taught) that only men were apostles.

There is an ambiguity in Paul's Greek at Romans 16:7; his use of the objective case includes both male and female. Brooten came to understand that Paul and his intended readers knew—as did Chrysostom and a millennium of subsequent Christians—that Junia was a woman who was an apostle "in Christ before me." But, she found, by about 1200 the fact of Junia being a woman was no longer mentioned. Apparently the church could no longer imagine that such a prominent early apostle was female, so the male form of the name *Junia* was created, even though there is no evidence in antiquity of the male form of that name!

So Martin Luther, writing in the early 1500s in his influential *Commentary on Romans,* assumed this apostle must be a man. By the 19th century Roman Catholic and Protestant scholars almost without exception spoke of Junias. And soon the maleness of all in the New Testament who were called apostles had become a further argument against the ordination of women to the priesthood.

"What reasons have commentators given for this change?" Brooten asks herself. "The answer is simple: a woman could not

Elizabeth Gibson Ferry

have been an apostle. Because a woman could not have been an apostle, the woman who is here called apostle could not have been a woman."[12]

Finally now, after Brooten's research and nearly 1600 years later, the *New Revised Standard Version* of the Bible has set this bit of the New Testament record straight. But the fact that a woman apostle was "erased" and converted to a male (and a correction was needed for the NRSV) is a tiny bit of profound evidence of the pervasive male resistance and unbelief about the role of women within the early church.[13]

Notice also what has happened to Mary Magdalene in Christian tradition. Mary Magdalene is one of the most prominent of these early Christian women and prominent in the gospels.[14] Yet the tradition subsequently portrayed her as a former prostitute. Elisabeth Moltmann-Wendel points out that this "tradition" about Mary Magdalene has no New Testament basis and is a subsequent fabrication.[15] This time it was a woman *so important* as a confidante of Jesus, a leader and a significant contender with Peter for prominence in the earliest Christian movement[16] that she could not be erased. So she was instead demeaned and trivialized by this attack upon her reputation.

Participants in the *Basileia* of God, God's Dawning New Age

The relevant category for Jesus does not seem to be whether someone is "created in the image of God" (as it is for the Church Fathers). What mattered to him is whether someone is participating in the *basileia* of God, God's dawning new age. Women are recorded in the gospel stories of Jesus' life and ministry as full participants in that new age, that *basileia.*

The gospel accounts tell of women being early recipients of the good news (gospel or *euangellion*) about Jesus as Messiah and Risen Lord. Women are reported to be hearing the Word of God and doing it. Women (as well as children and men and finally the dead) are being healed by Jesus, in what his followers saw as the

Elizabeth Gibson Ferry

signs of the presence in their midst of the power of God and God's *basileia.* Women are actively going and telling, witnessing, spreading the Word, converting others, and traveling about as disciples with Jesus' band. Then after his resurrection, women are described in Paul's letters and by Luke in The Book of Acts as being important leaders in the earliest Christian communities.[17]

"Woman, You Are Freed" (Luke 13:12)

Rachel Conrad Wahlberg notes that when Jesus healed the woman with the terribly bent back, he does not say, "You are healed," but instead he says, "Woman, you are freed."[18] Wahlberg says that Jesus frees women from "labels, limitations and low expectations."[19]

Therefore, if we take Jesus seriously, a new relationship between women and men emerges as a possibility. Relationships can be symmetrical and mutually empowering for both sexes because women and men are radically equal and equally active, just as the creative will of God intends us to be (Gen. 1:27). Fully freed women are not simply objects in others' lives but are fully human and active, thinking and feeling amd doing their days— "subject" in their own lives. Such women can be perceived by men as a serious threat to the masculine identity and social power of males. Tertullian at the end of the second century, Cyprian in the third, and Augustine in the late fourth century–all were Christian bishops who were important in shaping our Christian tradition, and who perceived and railed against women as just such a threat.[20]

But fully freed women can also be welcomed by secure males who are able to share power and can enjoy being companioned by equal and active women partners. Throughout his public career Bill Clinton has welcomed Hillary Rodham Clinton as a fully powerful co-architect of his political journey, while she has also maintained her own separately active and equal public and professional life. I once heard a man asked what was in it for men if women claim their power. His answer was startling in its simplicity: "It's a better tennis game with a better partner." Precisely!

4.

Jesus' Crucifixion

Making Jesus into a "Salvation Machine"

As a feminist I do not find the figure of Jesus in the four gospels problematic for women. What I do have difficulty with is what the church did after his death with the life, the persona, and the message of Jesus.

In his lifetime Jesus was a social and religious radical, breaking down prohibitions which worked against women, lepers (Luke 7:22), the sick (John 9:2), working on the Sabbath (Mark 2:27–28), healing on the Sabbath (Mark 3:1–5), and so on. His preaching centered on social justice (e.g., Luke 4:18–27; Matt. 6–7; Matt. 26:35–40).

But in the decades immediately after Jesus' death, the apostle Paul became the foremost interpreter of Jesus and a great missionary figure in the spread of what would become what we know as Christianity. Paul and most subsequent theologians centered not primarily upon Jesus' life and message but instead upon Jesus' death *and their interpretation of that death.*

Through their theologies of the cross, they made Jesus into a "salvation machine." They became obsessed with Jesus' death as a way of individual salvation. There was little or no social justice component to that message.

The "Blood on the Cross" Message of Individual Salvation

All that was the beginning of the "blood on the cross" message of individual salvation which I experienced in the Southern

Elizabeth Gibson Ferry

Baptist Church of my childhood. In the racially segregated South of that time, I knew people who could tell you the day and hour when they were "born again." But these same folk were totally oblivious to the great injustices of racist attitudes. They were supportive of the "Jim Crow laws" which created the legal basis for segregation. They were blind to the violence of lynchings and rape.

These white Christians celebrated the suffering of Christ's "passion" as salvific. But they did not see any connection of that suffering with the suffering of African-Americans.

Its lack of social justice, however, is not the only problem of the cross-obsessed preaching I grew up on. Certainly another major problem is in its underlying theology, which has focused so single-mindedly upon the cross itself. The cross, either in its starkly plain Protestant form or in its Orthodox and Catholic devotional form of the crucifix, has for centuries been the central icon of Christian faith and devotion. Jesus as the Christ "dying for our sins" is seen as the critical moment in salvation history. As someone has said, such theology is necrophilic, death-affirming rather than life-affirming.

A "Double Whammy" for Women

Feminist theologians writing in *Christianity, Patriarchy and Abuse* have focused on this glorification of suffering and self-sacrifice, especially as the theology of the cross combines with the social messages given to women. Joanne Carlson Brown and Rebecca Parker sum it up: "The central image of Christ on the cross as the savior of the world communicates the message that suffering is redemptive" and therefore it is implied that "our suffering for others will save the world."[1] And "this glorification of suffering as salvific, [is] held before us daily in the image of Jesus hanging from the cross."[2]

This honoring of Jesus' suffering may inspire a few men to heroic martyrdom—a few like Gandhi, Martin Luther King, Jr.

Elizabeth Gibson Ferry

and the archbishop of El Salvador, Oscar Romero. But for most men that glorification of suffering is more than blotted out by the culture's messages that men should live instead to further their own self-interest, power, career, money, and sexuality.

But the culture gives to women a different message than it gives men. Women are told, "Give yourself, submit yourself, Eve was created as a helpmate for Adam, and you should really live through taking care of your husband and children." It is a culture's call to self-sacrifice, a message intended however only for women.

Then on top of that message Christianity is teaching that to live a life of self-denial and self-sacrifice is to follow the way of the cross. And to do this is to find the experience which is at the heart of our salvation.

The "double whammy" for women is overwhelming. Making suffering sacred is, for women, an invitation to practice what feminist theologian Carter Heyward calls "theological masochism."[3] Or as Sheila Redmond says, "The focus on the need for redemption creates a sense of unworthiness and, eventually, guilt."[4]

So theologically-induced "bad feelings" are piled onto women's culturally-induced bad feelings about their second-class status and "evil" bodies. Little wonder then that feminists have identified low self-esteem as an important psychological problem for most women in this culture!

Seeing "That Old Rugged Cross" in a New Light

As women's voices have begun to be heard and women have started "naming the suffering, so as to begin the healing," women and also some men have begun to tell excruciating stories of childhood incest, physical and sexual abuse.

It is in this context that women are now taking a new and hard look at "that old rugged cross"—and what we see now is "divine child abuse," proclaimed as necessary and salvific. What we see is *not* Abraham's hand restrained by God from a sacrificial slaying of his son but instead God said to be for his own purposes *intentionally* killing a son. As Brown and Parker say, "To argue that salvation can only come through the cross is to make God a divine sadist and a divine child abuser."[5]

And if God abuses children, why shouldn't parents do this also? Philip Greven is an intellectual historian at Rutgers University. In his writing he traces the powerful and terrible intertwining of American Protestant colonial theology and the Calvinistic heritage of harsh physical abuse of children.[6] Brown and Parker say, "When parents have an image of a God righteously demanding the total obedience of 'his' son—even obedience to death—what will prevent the parent from engaging in divinely sanctioned child abuse,"[7] especially to force "obedience" to parental will?

"The image of God the father demanding and carrying out the suffering and death of his own son," Brown and Parker say, *"has sustained a culture of abuse and led to the abandonment of victims of abuse and oppression. Until this image is shattered, it will be almost impossible to create a just society."*[8]

This suggests a direction toward a just society which was never glimpsed by Walter Rauschenbush and the Social Gospel movement, *or* by Martin Luther King, Jr. and the Civil Rights movement, *or* by Reinhold Niebuhr and Christian ethical realism, *or* by World Council of Churches manifestos, *or* by the popes in their encyclicals. ***All these run aground in their attempts to come to grips with injustice because they do not comprehend their own faith-commitment to the glorification of violence in the cross.***

Creating a Fascination with Violence and Pain

The Swiss psychiatrist Alice Miller, in her book *For Your Own Good: Hidden Cruelty in Child-Rearing and the Roots of Violence,* explores the psychological processes by which the violence by one generation of parents, particularly fathers, toward their children begets in their sons of the next generation similar violence in turn toward their own children.[9] In three extended case studies she explores how childhood experiences of brutalization created monstrously violent and brutal adults.

In one of these cases, Miller examines all that is known of Adolf Hitler's early life. In his brutal treatment by his father she finds the psychological origins of his violence against Jews.

Then, Miller asks, how could one such "wounded" man, Adolf Hitler, reach by his speeches so quickly and so deeply into the emotions and psyche of an entire people, and win such total commitment to the Nazi cause?

Such a vast and rapid transformation was possible, Miller says, only because Hitler himself was a part of and also speaking to a nationwide population of adult survivors of childhood violence. Most of his German hearers had experienced childhood physical abuse similar to his own.[10]

The fact that the "Our-sin-is-laid-on-Him" atonement theology has for so many generations and centuries moved so many Christian hearts[11] raises an important question: Is this too a consequence of harsh and abusive physical discipline for children in Christian homes? Greven has gathered the historical records documenting a centuries-old tradition of such violence toward children among many Christian groups.[12] Had our own childhood been less violent, wouldn't we find the father-son violence inherent in Christian atonement theology either bizarre or repulsive?

When I was coming into teenage in my Southern Baptist religious context I could never understand why the "blood on the cross" theology (as I came to call it) *never* resonated in my spiritual being as did the truth of God's love manifested in the creation of the world. I knew the presence of that loving God in my own experience, "calling" me, upholding me, "visiting" me in translucent moments of God-encounter. Today I wonder if my lack of such resonance for "blood on the cross" came from my

Elizabeth Gibson Ferry

experience of a non-violent child-rearing, for which I am very grateful to my parents.

But those who do experience violent child-rearing add on other additional consequences. Childhood abuse catapults both genders into more extreme gender-stereotypic behavior. Girls become more docile and submissive women, easy candidates for further victimization. Boys become more aggressive and brutally violent men.[13]

A large proportion of men in prison for violent crimes (including rapists, murderers, serial killers) were themselves physically and/or sexually abused as children. Being abused or neglected as a child significantly increases the risk of being arrested for a violent crime.[14] It may come as news to advocates of "law and order" that probably the most effective thing we could do about stopping violent crime would be to stop fathers and grandfathers, uncles and older brothers, the man next door and the older boy next door, from physically and sexually abusing *male* children!

How are we to stop the abuse of children while at the same time our most sacred icon for religious contemplation is Jesus hanging on the cross, ordered there by his heavenly Father? Do you know the story of the young boy with behavior problems at school? He was sent from one school to another, finally becoming "good" in a parochial school. His grateful but curious parents (who were not Roman Catholic) asked him what was different about his new school, and he said, "Did you see that guy nailed to the wall? I figured that if God would do that to his own son, guess what He could do to me!"

5.

Changing an Entire Tradition

Making Women Visible

How do you take on a tradition that reflects the male image like a Narcissus pool, and re-make it over into a tradition that is also *in her image?*

The answer reminds me of the riddle about "How do two porcupines make love?" The answer is, "With difficulty!"— because the problem of the male-centeredness of the Christian tradition goes well beyond male generic language, biased history, and celibate theology. "You have to git man off your eyeball," as Shug suggests in *The Color Purple,* "before you can see anything a'tall."[1]

Some women feel that the only way to break the hold of that male image on our unconscious is to incorporate the female image of God into our theology and especially into our worship. They reason that imaging the great I AM in its female face (Goddess, Gaia, The Great Mother, Sophia, Wisdom, and so on) is the ultimate antidote to the denigration of women as inferior and evil. To see the female in the God-space cracks open the unconscious male imaging of God which is our deep legacy from thousands of years of patriarchy. As we learn to reverence the female in the divine, they argue, we are opened up to reverence the divine in the human female.

This is not a pathway that appeals to me. I feel it only compounds patriarchy's error in socially constructing God in its own gender image.[2] I cannot see that the Mystery of creative energy which has brought into being 193 billion galaxies has male form, and unfortunately for my participation in "the pathway of the Goddess," which seems so very meaningful to many women, I do not think it helpful philosophically or theologically to clothe that Creating Mystery now in female form, even in image or metaphor.

Cleansing the Temple

We may or may not add female images to the divine. But it is imperative, if we care about the psychic health of the young people we are rearing in our churches, that we *totally strip the male language/image/metaphor from our references to deity* in worship and in church life.

We must also *deconstruct the male-identified biblical text,* making clear the male voices of its authors and the male viewing points from which they speak. And we must *stop coating scripture with sacred varnish* in the pious words, "This is the Word of God." Instead, we must introduce patriarchal texts (or follow them) with prayers of repentance for the sin of the idolatry of the male which such texts embody.

We must do this to empower our girl children with affirmation. But we must do this also for our boy children, if we want them to be able to relate to the women in their lives (mothers, sisters, wives, colleagues, children) without the distorting filters of misogyny, which have for millennia beclouded and crippled male life-attitudes.

A Church Where Women Are Visible and Honored

In the 1970s our family attended Sunday services at the chapel of Wellesley College, the local women's college, under the pastorate of Paul Santmire. I gradually became aware how totally he had re-worked the quite traditional service.

When a hymn had no objectionable male language or meta-phor, we sang it from the hymnal. When we sang a hymn printed in the leaflet, it was because Paul had quietly reworked the words.

Then I began to realize that any illustration or anecdotes he used in sermons were all about women, never men. Paul was sensitive to the needs, expressed and unexpressed, of Wellesley College's students to have inclusive language and also to be visible themselves as a gender in his sermons. Finally, I realized that the stained glass windows in the Wellesley College chapel were all about women.

For too long we have expected women not to mind being invisible in our tradition. In our culture we have expected women to do the additional psychological work to "find themselves" in the male figures who are the main characters in the faith, the church, the culture, the stained-glass windows, and in the male-generic language and literature of our religious and national traditions.

Where Women Are Major Figures, Not Mere Bystanders

I remember a story told by Joseph Campbell, the great scholar of myths. He was teaching at Sarah Lawrence College and after a lecture about the mythic literature surrounding King Arthur, a woman student asked him about who in all the Arthurian saga she as a woman could identify with. Surprised, Campbell said that of course she could identify with the hero's mother, the hero's wife, the hero's sister, the hero's daughter. "No," the woman student said, "you don't understand!—*I want to be the hero.*"

There you have it. It is no longer sufficient for women to identify with the bystanders and the supporters in the hero's life. Women want to be the hero themselves. It is men's turn now to have to do the psychological work involved in "finding them-selves" in a heroic figure of the other gender, the heroic female.

What we want now are adulatory sermons and services about Mary Magdalene. Like Peter she was a prominent early Christian leader—and one of Jesus' closest friends. So she is a figure we all, both men and women, should try to emulate.

Let us celebrate the first apostle, the woman at the well. Can we, either male or female, be as effective an evangelizer as she was?

I want an Easter morning that says flat out that the men had all deserted, and only women witnessed and attested to the resurrection that Easter morn! I want stained glass windows that show the risen Christ surrounded by only those women!

And while we are at it, let us show the women who were present at the Last Supper, cooking in the kitchen. Someone has quipped, "If there was a meal, you better believe there were not just men present!"

I am also tired of looking at Christian art with Jesus in the center and a grouping of disciples "boundaried" by the male gender. This is *not* true to the gospel records or The Acts of the Apostles.

Church Life as a Massive "Latent Curriculum"

We have a huge job to open up not only the language but also the stained glass windows, the preaching, the story telling, the celebrating. We need this opening up because *everything* in the life of the church is a learning experience for us as adults as well as for children. Church life itself is a *massive latent curriculum* in which everything that happens is teaching someone something.

So we need to *never* refer to Abraham without also naming Sarah and Hagar, never refer to Isaac without Rebecca, and so on. When we talk about Francis of Assisi, we need also to talk about Hildegard of Bingen—who left a considerably larger literature about her own form of creation spirituality, a literature neglected by Christians for centuries!

What I want is that at least half of every worship service and every curriculum makes women as visible as men—the women of the Bible and the New Testament, the women in church

Penny Jackim/Ahimsa Graphics.
Permission of the artist.

history, and the women and women's issues in contemporary life. Women are half the human species. "Women hold up half the sky," as a Chinese saying puts it, and we will no longer be invisible and marginalized in church worship or preaching or in church lore—or in curricula.

A Celebration of Women

When I was growing up in my Southern Baptist Church, every fall and spring our church had an in-gathering to benefit overseas missions. As a young child I would go with my mother early in the morning to the huge kitchen in the church's basement. While the women of the church cooked, the janitor set up long tables and we children rolled out the long paper tablecloths and set the tables with the silver and glasses, salt, pepper, sugar and paper napkins.

It was a big operation involving many people, and at dinner time 300 to 400 men and women and children gathered in our church to eat a festival meal and to celebrate the memory of two great missionary figures, Lottie Moon in the fall, and Ann Judson in the spring. We were celebrating *women* as heroic religious figures! After dessert had been served I heard both men and women (including our much revered pastor) praise and eulogize a woman, either Lottie Moon or Ann Judson, who had heard and followed the call of God to Christian service.

I look back now on this and I realize how important those celebrations of women were in shaping my life. I concluded as a young girl that if I chose in my life to respond to the call of God, my home religious community would applaud and honor me as they had honored Lottie Moon and Ann Judson year after year.

Changing a Tradition of Celebrating Men

I still find it sad that males, when they created a religious system around themselves, chose primarily to honor what it is *men* do. How else are you to explain the fact that women's experience of giving birth has *never* been honored as sacred (even though it brings new life and the only on-going life our species knows in time)? Instead, women's natural bodily functions of menstruation and giving birth were declared "unclean" and "defiling" to the religious sanctuary.

Jesus honored women's giving birth and spoke of the new life we are called to as "being born again."[3] But the male-dominated tradition seized upon Jesus' words and used them to create male *imitation-births,* calling the "baptism" of infants their *true* birth, the time when they are "born again, into the family of God." This, it is implied, is the being born which really counts, *not* the birth from one's own mother. But ask yourself, "In which birth did God actually give you the gift of life?"

Mary Daly, in her scathing satire of the Looking Glass,[4] made many women aware of how the sacred rituals done by males *imitate* and *co-opt* many of women's sacred life-experiences. The feeding which women do at home became the communion presided over by men at church, and so on.

Going Beyond the Ancient and Crippling Hatred of Women

I say that it is time now to go back and re-sacralize these women's experiences which male religion has imitated and co-opted, and to do it with new and fresh eyes. To do less is to dishonor God's creation of woman. We can be filled with the spirit of Jesus, our founder, and be no longer stuffed with the ancient and crippling hatred of women which has dominated our woman-denigrating tradition.

I want ritual that celebrates the sacredness of women giving birth. I want to celebrate in church not just Mary birthing Jesus but all women birthing all children. I want to expand the traditional celebration of the Advent season and Christmas to celebrate the sacredness of women's bodies—not just women's wombs but women's breasts, vaginas, vulvas, clitorises—all that

God has provided to us as women and without which no human generations continue to be born on this Earth.

We do not have to image the godhead as female in order to celebrate the God-given natural body of the woman. I am convinced this celebration has already begun in our extensive use in our Christmas celebrations of wreaths, which (let's face it) are *not* celebrations, as I was once told, of the Alpha and Omega—but celebrations of the rounded circle of the woman's vagina, which makes birth (including Jesus' birth) possible.

I want curricula which point out the absurdity of the story of Eve born out of Adam's body (thus reversing what happens in natural birth where men *always* come out of women's bodies). I want curricula which make clear the misogyny in the Genesis 2 account which labels women's natural pain in childbirth the result of Eve's "curse" for sin.

I want curricula to point out that while a baby is half the father's genes and half the mother's genes, once that DNA template or blueprint is formed, every molecule and atom of that growing embryo is built out of the real body and real blood of that gestating mother's body. This is how actual life is gestated and born in each of us.

I want church curricula to point out that modern biology has "revealed" to us that all fetal life is initially neutral—it can become either male or female. If at a certain time a triggering process occurs, this sets in motion the development of the male genitalia for the fetus. Without that triggering process the fetus goes on to become female. Aristotle and Thomas Aquinas and the Christian tradition for centuries had it backwards and wrong, thinking men (and Adam) came first and women were "deformed males." These mistaken speculations were used again and again to exclude women from priesthood and to put down women as "imperfect" while men were being touted as perfect. Modern biology has overturned all that erroneous theological speculation, and the church would now like to be able quietly to forget its centuries of derogating women in this way. But such a long

Claire Flanders

history of Christian misogyny cannot now simply be ignored; it must be corrected.

I also want curricula which honor the sacred feeding that comes from women's breasts. Breast milk is women's blood with the red blood cells removed, and it sustains life in infants and also passes on her precious antibodies. We as faithful Christians may be given pause when we realize that birthing women can say to their children in truth, not metaphor, the hallowed words of the communion service: "This is my body, given for you; this is my blood, the blood of life, given for you."

A Life-Affirming Tradition for Ourselves and Our Children

Jesus said, "I have come that you might have life, and have it more abundantly" (John 10:10). To be a life-affirming tradition, we must lay aside our sacralizing of death and suffering, and put the affirmation of life at the core of our tradition.

For Jesus as we know him from the Gospels, abundant life was social justice, a banquet feast to which everyone was invited (Luke 14:15–24; Matt. 22:1–14). Jesus' message and life continued a liberation tradition begun in Moses ("I have seen the affliction of my people"—Ex. 3:7) and continued in the 8th century prophets ("Let justice roll down like water"—Amos 5:2-4). The account in Luke's gospel of Jesus' first sermon in a synagogue tells us he read Isaiah 61:1–2, "He has sent me to proclaim release to the captives and recovering of sight to the blind, to set at liberty those who are oppressed, to proclaim the acceptable year of the Lord" (Luke 4:18–20). Of the discipleship of caring which he expected from his followers, he said, "I was hungry . . . thirsty . . . a stranger . . . naked . . . sick . . . in prison. As you did it to one of the least of these my brethren, you did it to me" (Matt. 25:31–46).

I want a Christian education which focuses on the historical Jesus and his startling message of liberation and diversity and inclusion, because that message and example would be relevant

in a positive way to our contemporary struggles with racism, sexism, heterosexism, classism, and speciesism. Can we help Christian young people, both female and male, to imagine who Jesus—with his startlingly inclusive patterns of relating to women, the poor, the outcast, the marginalized—calls upon *us* to include in our Christian communities?

I also want a Christian education that is body-affirming and sexuality-affirming. And I would also like us to honor the body of the Earth. Sallie McFague's book *The Body of God*[5] is pointing us in this direction, toward images of God which are neither anthropomorphically male nor female, but which include and affirm the diversity and wonder of this entire created life-system of which we are *but one part.*

Can We Leave Behind Hierarchy?

Can we invent a Christian education which does not *assume,* and therefore teach, hierarchy (men over women, humans over other species, humans over nature and the planet, God over all)? Can we learn to teach, with reverence, the biospheral cycles of the Earth when we teach creation? To teach about the creation of the Earth in this way is to say that our created world came not by God's verbal fiat (Genesis 1) but by the Creator's incredible participation in billions of years of an evolutionary process. It is this process which has given rise to our present biological and ecological existence as selves in bodies within a natural context we call the living Earth-system.

Can we internalize God's concern for other species in this Earth-system as well as for us? (There are fragments in our heritage which suggest this: "When the rainbow is in the clouds, I will look upon it and remember the everlasting covenant between God and *every living creature* of all flesh *that is upon the Earth*" [Gen. 9:16].)

Can we discover the *"creation-based value"* of every species, which is established in that covenant with the entire creation, a

Claire Flanders

creation of which we are only a part, and not its Lord and Master? Can we climb down from the high illusion we have of ourselves as "king of the castle" and in "dominion" over all the other species?

Can we write some curricula filled with real biological data about our Earth and our life-partners on it, as well as with some genuine theological humility about our place in the divine scheme of things? We talk about humility as a Christian virtue, but it has seldom been practiced in our theology!

Can we teach Jesus in Christian education in a way that would make it obvious to our children that they should be "in solidarity with the poor"? Can we take Jesus' death away from those who would climb to heaven on his drops of blood? Can we finally see Jesus' death as what happened to a social revolutionary—and call our young people to the struggle against many oppressions, instead of focusing only on the dying?

Joanne Carlson Brown and Rebecca Parker have written, "We do not need to be saved by Jesus' death from some original sin. We need to be liberated from the oppression of racism, classism, and sexism, that is, from patriarchy."[6]

Fruits of the Patriarchal Spirit

The patriarchy of male power over female submission has done great harm by imposing itself upon Christian theology. This same patriarchal pattern also permeates male/female power relationships in the family. Much of the resulting harm in families has been hidden and is only now coming to light. Again, the daunting question is: Can we change the power relationships between male and female in the Christian family?

Patterns of wife-beating have been legitimated by the patriarchal imbalance of power, and validated by scripture.[7] The classic biblical text on the subject is from the apostle Paul: "Wives, be subject to your husbands, as to the Lord. For the husband is the head of the wife as Christ is the head of the church, his body, and is himself its Savior. As the church is subject to Christ, so let wives also be subject in everything to their husbands" (Eph. 5: 22–4). The most important 20th century Protestant theologian Karl Barth voiced similar views: "Woman is ontologically subordinate to man."[8]

But this is woman. What happens to children within these skewed power relationships in the Christian family? Judith Lewis Herman's ground-breaking work in *Father-Daughter Incest* highlights the profile of the incestuous father as being a pillar of the church, a pillar of the community.[9] She also is clear that the common thread in the profile of the abuser is the imbalance of power between the father and the mother.[10]

The religious issues of incest survivors are explored empirically in *Christianity and Incest,* by Annie Imbens and Ineke Jonker. Nineteen Dutch women, survivors, were reared as children in Holland in very Christian homes, both Protestant and Roman Catholic. Hear their voices, the voices of girl-children now grown to adulthood, speaking about their childhood sexual abuse which took place in Christian homes:

Question: *What aspects of religion did you experience as oppressive?*

Answer: Obedience, and that as a woman, you were always inferior to a man. You had to be subservient all the time, self-sacrificing.[11]

Question: *What connection do you see with religion?*

Answer: My father had very "Christian" ideas about women: women were supposed to be submissive, obedient, and servile. I used to wonder how incest could happen in such religious families. Now I think that families who practice their religion so strictly live in a closed system, a vacuum. . . . My father was religiously dogmatic. A certain image of women was fostered by the church, which enabled men to treat their women that way.[12]

Question: *What aspects of religion did you experience as oppressive?*

Claire Flanders

Answer: My father often said the commandment: "Honor thy father and thy mother." . . . I was completely abandoned to his will because I obeyed those commandments.[13]

Question: *What connection do you see with religion?*

Answer: Sometimes I asked my father why he kept making me do this. Then he said, "All women are the same as that first woman, Eve. You tempt me. In your heart, this is what you want, just like Eve." I used to pray "God, let it stop!" But God didn't intervene, so I thought, either it really was God's will, or I really was as bad as they said, and this was my punishment.[14]

Question: *What do you associate with these words?: Forgiveness.*

Answer: *Forgiveness*—that was the worst. I had to forgive him "70 times 70 times." It can't be forgiven, even if he were to ask for it—but he never has—even then I couldn't talk about forgiveness. He was a grown man, wasn't he? I was just a child.[15]

Perhaps now we will understand this summary statement by Imbens and Jonker: ***"Sexual abuse of children is the ultimate consequence of the gender power relations in our society that we call normal."***[16] And it is precisely these gender power relations which, from Ephesians to Karl Barth, Christian spokesmen have declared not only normal but God-given and ontologically established.

"I Was Just A Child"

Such haunting, poignant words! But they fill our hearts with the realization that we have been teaching our children power relationships which are simply sick. These teachings poison us and wound deeply. Sometimes it is as brutal as incest. Sometimes it is as quiet as the devastated lives of women silenced and stunted, women whose potential and promise given them in their God-given DNA, is never allowed to flower into anything approaching the full expression of their talents.

Claire Flanders

And then there are all the young boys, who grow into men poisoned into arrogance and male entitlement—and into abuse. What we have done is poison the well from which our children drink.

"I was just a child." This is no mere child's play, this need for a feminist Christian education which teaches and models equality and not hierarchy in the Christian family and the so-called "family of the church." This is deadly serious, because the harvest of the past in pain and stunted lives is very real, and has been carefully hidden and silenced, with Christianity as its powerful accomplice.

You cannot have a children-friendly tradition until you have a woman-respecting tradition. You cannot affirm life, without affirming women, and you cannot raise whole and life-affirming children without affirming women because children love their mothers, and need to be nurtured by them. Therefore it hurts children when Christian theology, ritual, and praxis denigrate and abuse their mothers—just as it hurts children to watch battering husbands/fathers beating their mothers.[17]

"I was just a child." Jesus said, "Let the little children come to me. Do not stop them, for it is to such that the *basileia* of God belongs" (Mark 10:14 NRSV). And again, "If any of you put a stumbling block before one of these little ones who believe in me, it would be better for you if a great millstone were fastened around your neck and you were drowned in the depth of the sea" (Matt. 18:6 NRSV).

How about a new commandment which says, "Honor the children, not the parents"? How about an Eleventh Commandment which says, "Thou shalt not commit incest."[18] How about a commandment that says, "Spare the child and throw away the rod"?[19]

"I was just a child." Do we care enough about our children in an emerging feminist world to challenge all the powerful men and the male-identified women in our Protestant and Roman Catholic traditions to really make the changes necessary to raise our

Elizabeth Gibson Ferry

children in a healthy, life-affirming and woman-affirming tradition? I don't know.

Another Reformation

What I am calling for is another Reformation of Christendom, freeing us this time not from the power of pope and priest but from the power of patriarchal males whatever their position. To urge this is to challenge nearly all of our tradition, and it is an awesome challenge. And a part of me fears for the challenge and also for the response.

"It is essential that our religious ideas and images function to heal and empower us, rather than reinforce the dynamics of self-denial, self-hate, child abuse and oppression," writes Rita Nakashima Brock.[20] In these words she says it all. Our Christian tradition—its ideas, ritual, theology, practice *and its Christian education*—must "function to heal and empower us." That is what our Creator had in mind for us. That is what the Jesus who called the children to him certainly had in mind.

Feminism is God's call to us, in this generation, to open up to radical change so that our tradition may be true again to Jesus, and become life-affirming for all.

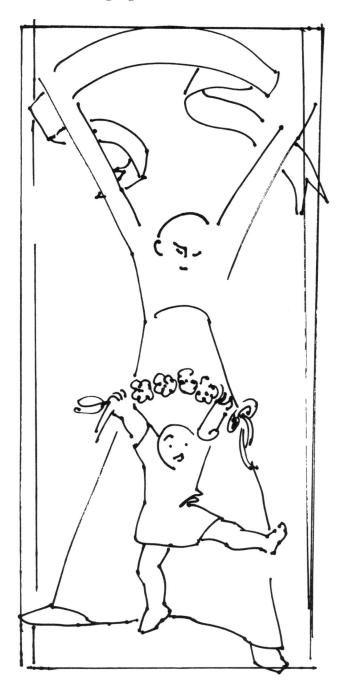

Elizabeth Gibson Ferry

Notes

Chapter 1. Theology through "Male-Colored" Glasses

1. Peter L. Berger, *The Sacred Canopy: Elements of a Sociological Theory of Religion* (Garden City, NY: Anchor, Doubleday, 1969 [1967]), p. 33.

2. For a survey and summary of this history, from pre-Christian times in the classical world to the present day, see Rosemary Radford Ruether, *Gaia and God: An Ecofeminist Theology of Earth Healing* (San Francisco: HarperSanFrancisco, HarperCollins, 1992), especially pp. 115-201.

3. God's statement of self-revelation to Moses, "I am who I am"— or "I will be whoever I will be" (Ex. 3:14), is interpreted by Thomas Aquinas in *Summa Theologiae* (I q. 13, a. 11; also Scg I. 22, par. 10) as "*He* who is," as if this were God revealing to Moses the maleness of God's ontological nature. See Elizabeth A. Johnson, *She Who Is: The Mystery of God in Feminist Theological Discourse* (New York: Crossroad, 1992), p. 241–3.

Chapter 2. The Denigration of Women

1. Jane Dempsey Douglass, "The Historian of Theology and the Witnesses." Nathaniel Taylor lectures, Yale Divinity School, 1990. The quotations are transcribed from tapes of the lectures.

2. Uta Ranke-Heinemann, *Eunuchs for the Kingdom of Heaven: Women, Sexuality and the Catholic Church,* trans. Peter Heinegg (New York: Doubleday, 1990), p. 187.

3. Ranke-Heinemann, p. 188.

4. Gregory of Tours, *History of the Franks,* trans. O.M. Dalton. (Oxford: At the Clarendon Press, 1927), 8, 20, pp. 344–5; also Charles Joseph Hefele, *A History of the Councils of the Church from the Original Documents,* trans. William R. Clark, vol. 4 (451–680 AD) (Edinburgh: T.& T. Clark, 1895), p. 406–9.

5. Margaret R. Miles, *Carnal Knowing: Female Nakedness and Religious Meaning in the Christian West* (Boston: Beacon Press, 1989), p. 162; see also Maryanne Cline Horowitz, "The Image of God in Man—Is Woman Included?" *Harvard Theological Review* 72: 3-4 (July-October 1979): 175–206.

6. Tertullian, "On the Apparel of Women," in *The Ante-Nicene Fathers: Translations of the Fathers Down to A.D. 325,* eds. Alexander Roberts and James Donaldson (Buffalo: Christian Literature, 1885), vol. 4, p. 14.

7. Miles, p. 160–1.

8. Miles, p. 152.

9. Miles, p. 153.

10. Miles, pp. 153.

11. See Lev. 15:19–31; 12:1–8, and also the service for the "churching of women" ("Thanksgiving after Childbirth") in the Book of Common Prayer, 1928. pp. 305–7.

12. See Ranke-Heinemann, *Eunuchs for the Kingdom of Heaven* for booklength documentation of the lengthy tradition in Christianity of pronouncing sexual intercourse to be evil.

13. Samuel Laeuchli, *Power and Sexuality: The Emergence of Canon Law at the Synod of Elvira* (Philadelphia: Temple University Press, 1972), p. 104; cited in Carter Heyward, *Touching Our Strength: The Erotic as Power and the Love of God* (San Francisco: Harper & Row, 1989), p. 44.

14. Laeuchli, cited by Heyward, *Touching Our Strength,* p. 167n.

15. See, for example, Margaret R. Miles, *Desire and Delight: A New Reading of Augustine's Confessions* (New York: Crossroad, 1992).

16. Jakob Sprenger and Heinrich Institoris, *The Hammer of Witches* (1487), I Q. 6. The two were German Dominicans and Sprenger a professor of theology in Cologne. Pope Innocent VII appointed Sprenger and Institoris as inquisitors of heresy in his "Witches Bull" of 1484. *The Hammer of Witches* is intended to be a commentary upon the "Witches Bull." (Ranke-Heinemann, pp. 238, 229, 235).

17. Feminists today argue that these crimes should be tried and punished as crimes of "power" and "violence." But such crimes also involve sexual lust out of control. So in seeking to *understand* such crimes, I feel that the sexual component of both the motivation and the crime cannot be ignored.

18. An interesting glimpse into the perennial problem of male sexual lust in the second through fifth centuries of the Christian Church in North Africa (Tertullian, Cyprian, Augustine) is provided by Margaret R. Miles. See "Patriarchy as Political Theology: The Establishment of North African Christianity" in *Civil Religion and Political Theology,* ed. Leroy S. Rouner (Notre Dame, Ind.: Boston University Studies in Philosophy and Religion, Vol. 8, University of Notre Dame Press, 1986), pp. 169–186. See also her *Desire and Delight.*

19. Rosemary Radford Ruether, "The Western Tradition and Violence Against Women," in *Christianity, Patriarchy and Abuse,* ed. Joanne Carlson Brown and Carole R. Bohn (New York: Pilgrim Press, 1989), p. 37.

20. For a detailed study see Lawrence Stone, *Family, Sex, and Marriage in England, 1500–1800* (New York: Harper Collins, 1983) and especially his later work based on a collection of documents Stone discovered late in his career from the Court of Arches, an ecclesiastical appeals court having jurisdiction over family cases from 1600 until 1857: *Road to Divorce: England 1530–1987* (New York: Oxford University Press, 1990) and two volumes of case studies, *Uncertain Unions: Marriage in England, 1660–1753* (New York: Oxford, 1992) and *Broken Lives: Separation and Divorce in England, 1660–1857* (New York: Oxford, 1993).

Chapter 3. Jesus and Women

1. See Rachel Conrad Wahlberg, *Jesus According to A Woman* (New York: Paulist Press, 1975) and *Jesus and the Freed Woman* (New York: Paulist Press, 1978).

2. Ranke-Heinemann, p. 120.

3. The only exception was an emergency, when a child or an animal was missing and must be found. See Pheme Perkins, *Jesus As Teacher* (Cambridge: At the University Press, 1990).

4. See Wahlberg, *Jesus According to a Woman,* pp. 43–47.

5. See, for example, Luke 1:5–25; also Gen. 16:1–2, 21:1–7.

6. Wahlberg, *Jesus According to a Woman,* pp. 43–47; also Elisabeth Schüssler Fiorenza, *In Memory of Her: A Feminist Theological Reconstruction of Christian Origins* (New York: Crossroad, 1983), p. 146.

7. The historical facticity of specific events in Jesus' life is a persistent concern of New Testament scholars. A tendency of the early church to embroider upon events to underscore its message, as in the Christmas narratives, is already evident in the gospels. This tendency became even more evident in the additional gospels which by the early 4th century the church had decided were not authoritative or "canonical."

8. Wahlberg, *Jesus According to a Woman,* pp. 31–41.

9. Wahlberg, *Jesus and the Freed Woman,* pp. 42–64.

10. Jesus' encounter with the Syrophoenician woman (Mark 7:25–30) is a possible exception. But note that this is also a memory of the only theological argument Jesus is ever recorded as conceding—and to a woman!

11. Bernadette Brooten, "'Junia . . . Outstanding among the Apostles' (Romans 16:7)" in *Women Priests: A Catholic Commentary on the Vatican Declaration,* ed. Leonard Swidler and Arlene Swidler (New York: Paulist Press, 1977), pp. 141–144.

12. Brooten, p. 142.

13. Such unbelief extended into the 20th century. Helmut Köster of Harvard Divinity School pointed out to me that Hans Lietzmann, the outstanding philologist of early 20th century New Testament studies, could not believe that the person named *Junias* could be a woman. "The name *Junias* is not in evidence anywhere else . . . the short form never occurs. But because this person so named is designated as an apostle, one has to posit that this was a man, even though the name *Junias* never occurs anyplace else in antiquity" *(An die Römer [Handbuch zum NT]*, 4th edition, [Tübingen, 1933 (1906)] p. 125—this passage translated by Helmut Köster).

14. Stories of Mary Magdalene were carried on by the Gnostic tradition in works dating into the second century, including *Gospel of Thomas, Dialogue of the Savior, Gospel of Philip, Gospel of Mary,* and *Pistis Sophia.*

15. Moltmann-Wendel, Elisabeth, *The Women Around Jesus,* trans. John Bowden (New York: Crossroad, 1982), p. 64–5.

16. See Schüssler Fiorenza, pp. 50–3.

17. For detailed study of the archeological and literary evidence, see Karen Jo Torjesen, *When Women Were Priests: Women's Leadership in the Early Church and the Scandal of their Subordination in the Rise of Christianity* (San Francisco: HarperSanFrancisco, 1993).

18. Wahlberg, *Jesus and the Freed Woman,* pp. 15–29.

19. Wahlberg, *Jesus and the Freed Woman,* p. 1.

20. See Margaret R. Miles, "Patriarchy as Political Theology."

Chapter 4. Jesus' Crucifixion

1. Joanne Carlson Brown and Rebecca Parker, "For God So Loved the World?" in *Christianity, Patriarchy and Abuse,* p. 2.

2. Brown and Parker, p. 8.

3. Carter Heyward, *The Redemption of God* (Washington, DC: University Press of America, 1982), p. 58.

4. Sheila A. Redmond, "Christian 'Virtues' and Recovery from Child Sexual Abuse," in *Christianity, Patriarchy and Abuse,* p. 77.

5. Brown and Parker, p. 23.

6. Philip Greven, *The Protestant Temperament: Patterns of Child-Rearing, Religious Experience, and the Self in Early America* (New York: Alfred A. Knopf, 1977); and *Spare the Child: The Religious Roots of Punishment and the Psychological Impact of Physical Abuse* (New York: Knopf, 1990).

7. Brown and Parker, p. 9.

8. Brown and Parker, p. 9.

9. Alice Miller, *For Your Own Good: Hidden Cruelty in Child-Rearing and the Roots of Violence* (New York: Farrar, Straus, Giroux, 1983), pp. 3–106.

10. Miller, *For Your Own Good,* pp. 142-197.

11. The *Messiah,* by George Frederick Handel gives us a window into this. See part 2—"Surely, He hath borne our griefs," "And with His stripes we are healed"—"All we like sheep have gone astray; we have turned every one to his own way. And the Lord hath laid on Him the iniquity of us all."—and just preceding the paean of praise in the Hallelujah chorus to "the Lord God Omnipotent" who "shall reign forever and ever," there is a celebration of God's righteous wrath and abusive power: "Thou shalt break them with a rod of iron; Thou shalt dash them in pieces like a potter's vessel"—and immediately the hallelujah celebration of God's power over all.

With new eyes we can see here the demand for total obedience by an authoritarian parent, the violence of an abusive father, and the induced guilt/shame of the abused child which becomes the "sin" laid upon Jesus.

12. Greven, *The Protestant Temperament.*

13. Elaine Hilberman Carmen, Patricia Perri Rieker and Trudy Mills, "Victims of Violence and Psychiatric Illness" *American Journal of Psychiatry* 141 (1984): 378–83 .

14. Cathy Spatz Widom, "The Cycle of Violence," *Science* 244 (1989): 160–6.

Chapter 5. Changing an Entire Tradition

1. Alice Walker, *The Color Purple* (New York: Washington Square Press, Simon & Schuster, 1982), p. 179.

2. See Elizabeth Dodson Gray, *Patriarchy as a Conceptual Trap* (Wellesley, Mass.: Roundtable Press, 1982).

3. See Jesus' dialogue with Nicodemus, John 3:1–10; also John 1:12–13.

4. Daly, p. 195–8.

5. Sallie McFague, *The Body of God* (Minneapolis: Augsburg Fortress, 1993).

6. Brown and Parker, p. 27.

7. Susan Brooks Thistlethwaite, "Battered Women and the Bible: From Subjection to Liberation," *Christianity and Crisis* (November 16, 1981): 308–13. Also R. Emerson Dobash and Russell Dobash, *Violence Against Wives* (New York: Free Press, 1979).

8. See Karl Barth, *Church Dogmatics*, ed. G. W. Bromiley and T. F. Torrance (Edinburgh: T. & C. Clark, 1956–1962). III/4, pp. 116–240. Of Barth's views Mary Daly writes, "Barth goes on and on about women's subordination to man, ordained by God. Although he goes through a quasi-infinite number of qualifications, using such jargon as 'mutual subordination,' he warns that we must not overlook the 'concrete subordination of woman to man' (p. 175). He writes 'Properly speaking, the business of woman, her task and function, is to actualize the fellowship in which man can only precede her, stimulating, leading, and inspiring. . . . To wish to replace him in this, or to do it with him, would be to wish not to be a woman.' In case the point is not clear, he adds the rhetorical question: 'What other choice has she [than to be second] seeing she can be nothing at all apart from this sequence and her place within it' (p. 171). This is justified as being the divine order, according to Barth." (Daly, *Beyond God the Father*, p. 202.)

9. Judith Lewis Herman with Lisa Hirschman, *Father-Daughter Incest* (Cambridge, Mass.: Harvard, 1981), pp. 71–2.

10. Herman, pp. 78–9.

11. Annie Imbens and Ineke Jonker, *Christianity and Incest* (Minneapolis: Fortress, 1992), p. 93.

12. Imbens and Jonker, pp. 39–40.

13. Imbens and Jonker, p. 40.

14. Imbens and Jonker, p. 66.

15. Imbens and Jonker, p. 34.

16. Imbens and Jonker, p. 119.

17. For the effect on children of male violence toward their mothers, see Renée McDonald and Ernest Jonriles, "Marital Aggression and Child Behavior Problems: Research Findings, Mechanisms and Intervention Strategies," in *Behavior Therapist* (1991): 189–192. Also Lisa Reiter-Lavery, "Children's Reactions to Witnessing Marital Violence," (student paper, Catholic University, 1991).

18. The Eleventh Commandment is a movement within Quaker congregations initiated by anthropologist Dana Raphael of Westport, CT.

19. This commandment is inspired by the work of Philip Greven. See his *Spare the Rod*.

20. Rita Nakashima Brock, "And a Little Child Will Lead Us: Christology and Child Abuse," in *Christianity, Patriarchy and Abuse*, p. 54.